④

1 CIRRO-CUMULUS
   (Mackerel sky)
2 CIRRUS *(Mares tails)*
3 CUMULUS
   (Fair weather clouds)
4 CUMULO-NIMBUS
   (Thunder clouds)

Series 536

Why does it rain? What can we learn from the clouds? What IS "a depression over Iceland?" How does a barometer work?

These are some of the questions answered in this beautiful little book about British weather. The skilfully prepared text and twenty-four full-page pictures and diagrams in colour explain clearly the causes of our climate and the principles of weather forecasting.

As a guide to the ever-interesting subject of the weather, or as a simple introduction to the science of meteorology, this splendid book will fascinate children—and their parents too.

The WEATHER

by
F. E. NEWING, B.Sc.
and
RICHARD BOWOOD

with illustrations by
ROBERT AYTON

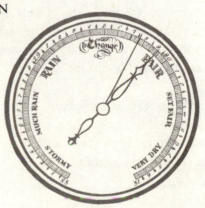

Ladybird Books Ltd Loughborough

The Earth's Atmosphere

The earth is enclosed in a layer of air, called the atmosphere, which extends upwards for approximately two hundred miles. This atmosphere, which is a mixture of gases, gets thinner, or less dense, as height increases, and there is hardly any at all fifty to sixty miles up. It is the movement of air within the atmosphere which brings different weather conditions.

The view of the earth's surface from outer space would show it covered with broken cloud at varying heights, as shown in the picture. Almost all this cloud is in the *lowest* layer of the atmosphere, called the troposphere, which extends upwards about ten miles from the earth's surface.

Above the troposphere is the stratosphere, some fifteen miles thick; then the mesosphere, which continues up perhaps for a further thirty miles; and finally the ionosphere, which goes to the outer edge of the atmosphere.

The movements of air which bring variations in the weather are caused by differences in temperature over the earth's surface, due to the heat of the sun. This is the main cause, but air movements are also complicated by the presence of large areas of land, mountains and oceans on the surface of the earth, and by the fact that the earth spins on its axis.

4

British Weather

The weather follows a set pattern in many parts of the world, and changes can be predicted months ahead. Every year rain, sunshine, particular winds or snow will arrive within a few days of the expected date.

We in the British Isles know only too well that our weather can never be depended upon. When the Meteorological Office makes its forecast it rarely predicts the weather for more than twenty-four hours ahead. We have warm days in winter, cold days in summer, and rain at any time. The farmer, whose work depends so much on the weather must "make hay while the sun shines". He has to be weather-wise, and the countryman has a store of traditional weather-lore and sayings.

The weather in the British Isles is changeable because of our geographical position, with the land mass of Europe and Asia on one side and the Atlantic Ocean on the other. The Arctic and the tropical regions are the sources of cold and warm air masses, which move to meet over the Atlantic Ocean. These movements are shown by the bands of colour on the map.

Each of these air masses carries with it its own kind of weather, and what happens when they meet over the Atlantic largely decides the weather of the British Isles.

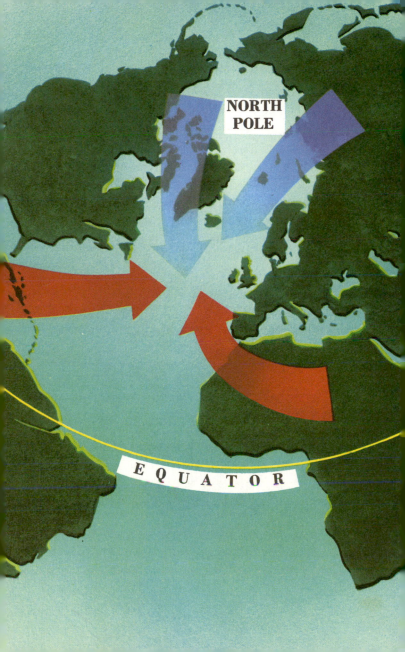

NORTH
POLE

EQUATOR

Why do the Winds Blow?

Wind is moving air, which brings various kinds of weather with it, according to its source.

The air moves from places where the air pressure is high to places where it is lower, and we often find that the pressure is lower over hot regions than it is over cooler. That is why a breeze will blow from the cool sea to the much warmer land on a hot and otherwise calm day. This is the sea breeze, or onshore breeze. At night, when the sea is warmer than the land, the breeze blows the other way, from land to sea.

The idea of high and lower pressure requires some explanation. If we want water to flow through a pipe we must either raise one end or put in a pump. Either way will produce high pressure at one end and low at the other. The water in the first case flows downhill; in the second case it flows from the high pressure created by the pump to the low pressure.

Air behaves in the same way as water and moves because of pressure differences. The greater the pressure—the faster the flow: so the bigger the difference in air pressure between two places the faster the air will move, or the stronger the wind will blow.

If, then, we can measure the pressure of the air in different places at the same time we can, to a certain extent, forecast the likely movements of the air and so make a start in predicting the weather.

The Barometer

The pressure of the atmosphere in any one place depends on the air above it, and this air is always changing. Sometimes it is more, and sometimes less dense, and this causes changes of pressure. The instrument which measures this changing pressure is the *barometer*.

There are two kinds. One is usually shaped like a banjo, and contains a long glass tube, shaped like the letter 'J' with one end open and the other sealed. This tube contains mercury. The dial has a scale which usually reads from 28 to 31 inches and a pointer moves round this scale. The dial reading is the difference in level, measured in inches, of the mercury in the two arms of the tube, and these levels change as the pressure of the air changes. The other kind of barometer shown is called an *aneroid*. This contains no liquid; instead the changing air pressure moves the top of a metal canister, and this movement operates the pointer.

The words on the dial—*Set Fair, Rain, Stormy, etc.*—do not in fact mean much; it is the movement of the pointer showing how the pressure is changing that gives a guide to the weather. A steadily rising barometer is an indication of improving weather, while a falling barometer usually means a change for the worse.

The barometer is often called a weather glass, but it really only tells us one of the many things which affect the weather—the pressure of the air.

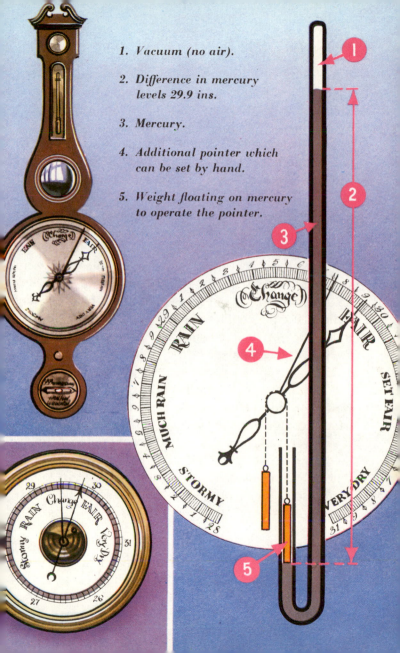

1. *Vacuum (no air).*

2. *Difference in mercury levels 29.9 ins.*

3. *Mercury.*

4. *Additional pointer which can be set by hand.*

5. *Weight floating on mercury to operate the pointer.*

Prevailing Winds

Air is moving (that is, winds are blowing) at both high and low levels in the atmosphere. The high level winds, blowing at ten miles or more up, are those met by air liners. At this height they say they are flying "above the weather", because it is the low level winds, much nearer the earth's surface, which are concerned with our weather.

A wind which blows steadily always in the same direction is called a prevailing wind. In the days of sailing ships certain of these prevailing winds which blew across the oceans were used by ships and were known as trade winds. The diagram shows how ships used these winds to sail to and from America. To-day airliners use the high level winds in much the same way, trying to plot their courses to make use of the high level prevailing winds.

Great Britain is just in the path of a prevailing south-westerly wind. (That means, of course, as always with wind directions, a wind blowing *from* the south-west.) If you were to keep a day by day record of the direction of the wind over a period of months you would find that it blew from one direction more than any other. In the south and west this would certainly be south-westerly.

If you look at trees and bushes in exposed places, especially on the coast, you will notice that they grow leaning away from the prevailing wind.

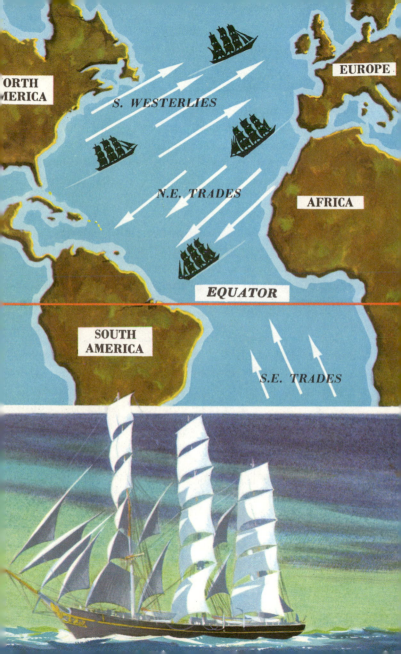

North, South, East and West Winds

A weather vane often tops a church spire, tower or high building. Whatever the design, they are made to turn in the wind so that they point to the direction from which it is coming. They are really only *wind* vanes. Just as the barometer only tells us the pressure of the air, so the weather vane only tells us the direction of the wind. Neither alone can tell us what the weather will be.

The weather vane can, however, give us some indication of the weather, because the direction of the wind is often associated with certain kinds of weather. There are no hard and fast rules—but, for example, the north wind is usually cold and the south wind warm.

The north wind is likely to be cold because it has come all the way from the ice of the polar regions. Winds from the south and south-west, on the other hand, are likely to be warm because they come from the warmer regions near the equator. Since they blow across the Atlantic Ocean they are usually moist, and may bring rain.

The west wind, too, comes across the ocean and can bring rain. The east wind blows across Europe and is frequently dry and often cold.

The weather vane in the picture shows the wind blowing from the south-west, and the clouds show that it will probably soon be raining.

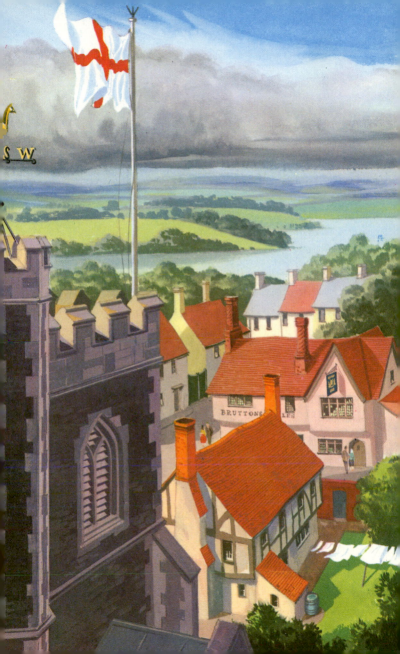

Measuring the Strength of the Wind

The speed of the wind is measured by an instrument called an anemometer, shown in the picture. The wind spins the cups, and the wind speed is registered on a dial below in miles per hour. It is important, of course, that the anemometer is used in an exposed position, where the wind is not broken by hills, woods or buildings.

You can make a simple anemometer. A piece of thick wire mounted on a baseboard carries a piece of card, such as a postcard, freely suspended by two wire rings. A curved scale is fitted to the upright so that as the card is blown upwards its edge moves over the scale. This is marked, by observation, over a period of time according to a simplified version of the Beaufort Scale, explained below.

The anemometer is put in the most exposed place available and pointed in the direction from which the wind is blowing, and the wind strength is read off the scale.

The Beaufort Scale is given on the next page. This classifies wind speeds in thirteen numbered groups, from 0 (Calm) to 12 (Hurricane). Thus a wind can be described by its Beaufort number—Force 3, Force 5, and so on. The scale of the home-made anemometer can be marked by observing the effects of the wind as shown in the fourth column on the next page.

THE BEAUFORT SCALE

Beaufort Number	Wind	M.P.H.	Effect over land
0	Calm	1	Smoke rises vertically
1	Light air	1- 3	Smoke drifts
2	Light breeze	4- 7	Leaves rustle, wind felt on face
3	Gentle breeze	8-12	Leaves move, light flag is extended
4	Moderate Breeze	13-18	Dust and loose paper blows about. Small branches move
5	Fresh breeze	19-24	Small trees sway a little
6	Strong breeze	25-31	Large branches sway, wires whistle
7	Moderate gale	32-38	Whole trees sway, hard to walk against the wind
8	Fresh gale	39-46	Twigs break off trees, very hard to walk into wind
9	Strong gale	47-54	Chimney pots and slates blown off. Large branches down
10	Whole gale	55-63	Trees uprooted, serious damage to buildings
11	Storm	64-72	Very rare inland, causes widespread damage
12	Hurricane	72 and more	Disastrous results

The wind strengths usually marked on the scale of a home-made anemometer are: 0, 1 and 2 = *Light;* 4 and 5 = *Moderate;* 6 = *Strong;* 7 = *High;* and 8 and 9 = *Gale.*

FORCE 0

FORCE 2

FORCE 5

FORCE 7

FORCE 8

FORCE 10

The Changing Course of the Wind

We have already seen that winds blow from high to low pressure areas. They do not, however, blow from one area to another in a straight line; they take a spiral course, just as bath water spirals down the plug hole. If we could look down on a low pressure area and see the wind, we should notice that it spirals in an anti-clockwise direction—in the opposite direction to the hands of a clock. Round a high pressure area, however, the wind circulates in the opposite direction—clockwise.

A low pressure area is called a depression, a word with which we are familiar from weather forecasts. These depressions generally develop over the Atlantic and usually travel eastwards across the British Isles, carrying their circulating wind systems with them. They vary in size, and may be a thousand miles across.

The diagrams show how the wind changes as a depression moves along. In position A, a depression is moving towards the observer. The wind, blowing anti-clockwise, appears to him to be blowing from the south-east. When the depression has travelled across him to position B (in second diagram), the wind has changed from the south-east and is blowing from the north-west.

There is a simple rule for finding the position of a depression known as 'Buys Ballot's Law'. Stand with your back to the wind, and the depression or low pressure area will be on your left hand.

Observer
Path of depression
Wind direction

DEPRESSION

DEPRESSION

Gales and Hurricanes

In the weather forecasts we sometimes hear that: "An intense depression is centred south of Iceland . . ." An 'intense depression' means an exceptionally low pressure in the centre of a wind system, with the barometer reading perhaps only about twenty-eight inches of mercury. Consequently the wind blowing into that depression will be strong. This particular forecast would be important to a fishing fleet in the area, which could expect to hear a gale warning.

Wind speeds are generally higher at sea than on land, because there are no mountains, hills, woods or buildings to break the force of the wind. A Force 6 wind on land could well be Force 8, or a 'fresh gale' at sea.

In the British Isles we rarely have winds stronger than Force 10, and even that is a very rare occurrence. A full gale is a very alarming experience, for the wind can uproot whole trees.

It is impossible for anyone who has not experienced a hurricane to imagine its tremendous force, capable of devastating whole areas. In a hurricane winds blow at seventy-two miles an hour and more, with gusts of more than one-hundred-and-twenty m.p.h.

At the centre of the very violent circulating wind of a hurricane there is an area of calm—'the eye of the hurricane'. When a hurricane crosses the course of a ship she will first encounter a most violent storm, then cross an area of calm and then sail through another violent storm—*with the wind blowing from the opposite direction.*

Water Vapour in the Air

In a 'weather house', shown in the picture, the lady comes out when it is likely to be fine and the man when it is likely to rain. This and other simple devices, the donkey with the blue tail, the fir cone and the piece of seaweed all tell the same thing, the amount of water vapour in the air, or the *humidity* of the air. It is more likely to rain when the humidity of the air is high than when it is low, so the weather house does give a guide to the weather.

Water vapour is always present in the air and it is completely invisible. It comes from water on the earth's surface—in seas, lakes, rivers and puddles—which is changed into vapour by heat from the sun. This process of *evaporation* is helped by the wind. That is why the washing dries better on a warm, breezy day.

Water vapour can change back into water, or *condense*, and when this happens clouds are formed. The clouds move with the wind, and under certain conditions (as explained on the next page), the water returns to the earth as rain. It is then ready to evaporate again to continue the everlasting process.

The Meteorologist measures the amount of water vapour in the air, or the humidity, with an instrument called a hygrometer, which is shown in the picture. The weather house, the donkey, the fir cone and the seaweed are all simple hygrometers.

WEATHER HOUSE

THE WEATHER HOUSE

The lady and the man are suspended by a piece of catgut, which twists and untwists as the humidity of the air changes. This brings the lady out in fine weather and the man out when rain is likely.

WET AND DRY BULB HYGROMETER

The wet bulb is surrounded by a wick dipping into a pot of water, so that it is always damp. If the air is dry, water from the wick evaporates rapidly and cools the bulb, so that this thermometer shows a lower temperature than the dry bulb. If the air is humid, there is little evaporation and little cooling so the two thermometers register almost the same temperature. From the two temperatures the meteorologist can calculate the humidity of the air.

Why does it Rain ?

The precise causes of rainfall are very complicated and are not fully understood even by meteorologists, but the general idea is simple enough. When air carrying the invisible water vapour is cooled, the vapour condenses to form tiny droplets of water so small that they float in the air and are visible as cloud or mist. When the droplets join together they become heavier, and fall—as rain.

How does the moving air get cooled? In general the temperature of the air falls as height increases, so if air is forced upwards it cools. The picture shows three of the ways this can happen.

In the first diagram the shape of the land causes the air to cool, for a range of hills forces the warm air upwards. The second diagram shows what happens when a mass of warm air meets a mass of cold air. The warm air, being less dense, floats upwards over the wedge of cold air, and is consequently cooled.

In the third diagram the air is warmed when it comes into contact with an area of ground which is hotter than its surroundings—the town in the diagram. The air expands, becomes less dense and so it rises, and cools.

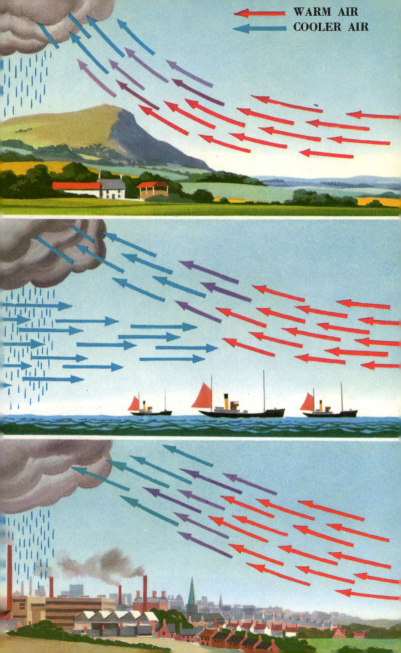

WARM AIR

COOLER AIR

How Much does it Rain ?

Rainfall is measured and recorded with a rain gauge, which consists of a funnel leading into a bottle. At regular times the rainwater is poured into a specially marked tube which measures the rainfall accurately in inches.

You can record the rainfall where you live by making a simple rain gauge. There is a difficulty, however, for unless your funnel and tube are specially made your results will not be in inches of rain. But you can still keep a record and compare the rainfall from day to day, not in inches but in your own units of rainfall.

Meteorological records show that different parts of the British Isles have very different rainfall. In London, and Eastern England, the average rainfall in a year is twenty-four inches; in Aberystwyth in Wales it is forty-six inches; and around Ben Nevis in Scotland it is one-hundred-and-sixty-one inches.

The map shows clearly that the heaviest rainfall (shaded blue) is in the mountainous parts, where the prevailing winds from the west and south-west are forced upwards. These winds, blowing from the Atlantic Ocean, often carry a great deal of water vapour, which accounts for the heavy rainfall. By the time they reach the eastern side of the country they have lost some of their moisture, and this is one of the reasons why the eastern side is much drier.

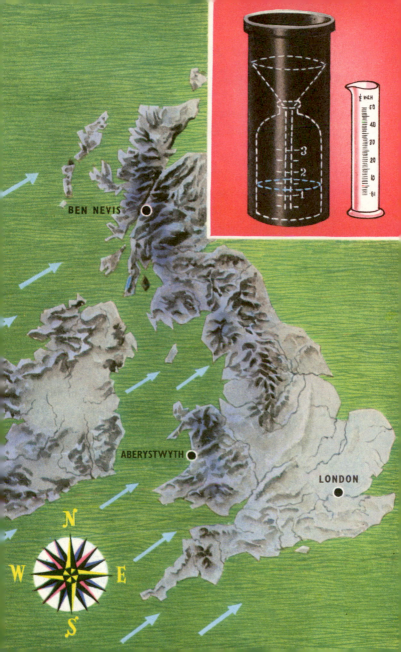

BEN NEVIS

ABERYSTWYTH

LONDON

N
W E
S

½ INCH
50
40
30
20
10

Snow, Sleet and Hail

We have seen on page 26 that when water vapour condenses the droplets may turn to rain. This is not, of course, the only form in which water returns to the earth; it can also fall as snow, sleet or hail—all forms of ice.

If the rising air carrying water vapour cools to below freezing point tiny ice crystals are formed instead of droplets of water. The crystals grow in the cloud, cluster together and form snow flakes which fall gently to the earth. The snow crystals are always six-pointed stars, but it is most unlikely that any two snow flakes will be *exactly* the same.

When it is very cold the flakes are small, but if it is only just about freezing they will be large and soft. Some may melt before they reach the ground, in which case we have sleet.

Snow and sleet belong to winter but hail often falls in summer time. Rapidly rising columns of warm air, which occur in the summer, can build up very tall clouds, which are very cold at the top so that ice crystals form. The crystals fall through the cloud until they meet water droplets moving up. The droplets freeze on to the crystals, building a layer of ice, and if the air currents are strong enough the hail stones are carried up and down through the cloud, getting larger each time, until they fall to earth. The ice crystals in the picture are magnified twenty-five times, and there could be about two hundred of them in a single snow flake.

Dew and Frost, Mist and Fog

Dew and frost both occur on still clear nights. Heavy dews usually follow warm days during which a great deal of water is evaporated into the air from streams, lakes and puddles. When the sun sets, the ground cools rapidly if there is no cloud, and so does the layer of air close to it. Some of the water vapour in this layer condenses and forms dew.

When the ground and the layer of air close to it cool below freezing point, the water vapour condenses as ice crystals, or frost.

Mist, like cloud, is made of tiny droplets of water; but while clouds are formed by the cooling of rising air, mist forms when warm air is cooled by contact with cold air close to the ground. Mist occurs more frequently in river valleys, along streams or over lakes, because the air has become saturated with water vapour by evaporation. The mist we see round mountains, hills and high ground is really low cloud.

Fog is a thick mist and is formed in just the same way. In big towns water droplets form very easily round the particles of soot and dust which are present in the air, and this can result in a very thick and dirty fog.

At sea, mist or fog is caused by warm air blowing over the cooler water of the sea.

Mists often clear quickly when the sun rises, as the water in them evaporates again.

Clouds and Cloud Formations

If we want to know if it is going to rain, or whether the rain is likely to stop, we look up at the clouds. Most of us can tell a rain cloud, but the skilled observer, can tell a great deal more from the clouds, and from the way they change.

There are three main types of cloud, which were first named in the year 1803 by the English chemist Luke Howard, a pioneer of meteorology. The types he named were *Cirrus*, *Cumulus* and *Stratus*.

CIRRUS CLOUDS. These are usually high and appear as delicate threads of whitish cloud against a blue sky. Because of their height they are composed of ice crystals and not of water droplets.

The picture shows a typical kind of cirrus cloud, often called 'Mares' Tails' because the wisps of cloud look like the tails of flying horses. These often mean a change in the weather, which is why the farmer is hurrying to get in his hay.

CUMULUS CLOUDS. These are heaped or piled-up clouds which look like great fluffy balls of cotton-wool, with tops like cauliflowers and flat bases. They are usually brilliant white in the sunshine, and sometimes tower up to great heights. (See picture opposite page 36.)

STRATUS CLOUDS. These are layers of cloud which can form at any height and tend to cover the whole sky. (See picture opposite page 38.)

Cumulus Clouds

The picture shows two sorts of cumulus cloud which might be seen on a summer's day. They all have the rounded appearance typical of this cloud form. At the top left are 'fair weather cumuli', fluffy at the top and flat at the base, moving steadily with the wind. In the centre a cumulus cloud is building up, or boiling up, to a great height where there is a rapidly rising current of air.

The tops of these towering clouds sometimes reach twenty-thousand feet and may then spread out to form the anvil shape of the cloud in the centre. When clouds like these begin to form on a hot summer day they usually mean thunder storms, with hail and rain by the evening. This is the storm-cloud, in which hailstones and large raindrops are formed. There is an old saying about this kind of cloud—"Mountains in the morning, Fountains in the evening".

When the rounded cumulus clouds appear very high in the sky, in the cirrus cloud region, they are called *cirro-cumulus*. Similarly, cumulus clouds at medium height in the sky are called *alto-cumulus*, *alto* meaning in this case medium. Sometimes cumulus clouds form a wide layer in the sky at fairly low levels, and then they are called *strato-cumulus*, *stratus* meaning a layer.

One type of high cumulus, which gives the appearance of the scales of a fish, is called a 'mackerel sky' and means changeable weather.

Stratus Cloud

Cloud in layers is called *stratus* and in the picture we see low stratus cloud; the sky is overcast and the sun probably concealed. Through a break in the stratus a higher layer can be seen, made up of cumulus clouds, and therefore called *strato-cumulus*.

The spreading of a cloud sheet across the sky often means that the weather is going to change for the worse. The first sign comes from the highest clouds, when cirrus cloud begins to spread and form a thin milky layer called *cirro-stratus*. As the bad weather approaches, the cloud layer gradually comes down until finally the sky is quite overcast by very low grey cloud, from which we get continuous rain or snow. This is the most unpleasant kind of stratus cloud, called *nimbo-stratus*, *nimbus* meaning a cloud, and usually a rain cloud.

We who live in the British Isles may often grumble at our changeable weather, but we are fortunate in the infinite variety of the clouds in our sky. The ever-changing cloud formations are an exciting part of the scenery, in the country or at the seaside. Clouds can be very beautiful; at sunrise or sunset, or when they race across the moon, or at any time of any day.

Thunder and Lightning

Thunder storms can and do occur at any time of the year, and in any part of the country. They sometimes provide us with a wonderful firework display which we can enjoy without anxiety, though it is not wise to shelter under a tree during a storm.

For a thunder storm to develop there must be plenty of water vapour, or high humidity, in the lower layers of air, and this must cool quickly as it rises. On page 36 we saw how cumulus clouds can build straight up and spread out to form an 'anvil'. This is the thunder cloud, or *cumulo-nimbus*.

Inside this cloud raindrops, and perhaps hailstones, are moving up and down and these help to produce electric charges in different parts of the cloud. Eventually the difference in electrical pressure between various parts of the cloud may reach several millions of volts, and then enormous sparks will flash from one place in the cloud to another, or from the cloud to the earth.

This lightning flash heats the air to white heat, so that it expands very rapidly to produce the sound wave which we hear as thunder.

We see the lightning at once, but the sound takes about five seconds to travel a mile, so if we count slowly between seeing the lightning and hearing the thunder we can work out how far away the storm is.

Sunshine and Sunshine Records

The sun, of course, is always shining though it is often partly or completely obscured from us by cloud. Fortunately the light and warmth from the sun are not entirely stopped by the clouds, so the growth of plants and the evaporation of water continues normally.

Meteorologists keep records of sunshine as they do of everything else connected with the weather. The sunshine recorder is a glass ball with a curved strip of paper below it. When the sun shines its heat rays are focused by the ball on to the paper and scorch it. If the sun shines all day a continuous scorch line is made across the paper as the sun moves across the sky. If, however, there is only occasional sunshine the paper shows a series of scorch lines which added together give the total hours of sunshine in the day.

Smoke and haze often cut down the sunshine in large industrial cities to a considerable extent. The country and the seaside, which are usually free from smoke, have much better sunshine records.

Sunshine recorders are frequently seen at seaside resorts, because a good sunshine record is an important attraction to holidaymakers. Sunshine does us good, and it makes us feel good, too.

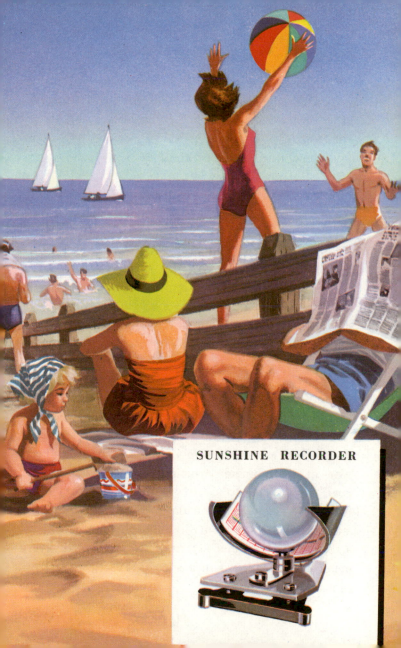

SUNSHINE RECORDER

Measuring Temperature

The meteorologist must know the temperature of the air. This is measured by a *thermometer* in degrees, either on the Fahrenheit or Centigrade scale (F. or C.). The freezing point of water is 32°F. or 0°C. A summer day temperature could be about 80°F., which is nearly 27°C. But on a cold winter day it could be 25°F., or almost – 4°C. Temperatures are always recorded in the shade, out of the direct rays of the sun.

For recording the highest and lowest temperatures reached in a period, usually twenty-four hours, a *maximum and minimum* thermometer is used (4). On this the highest and lowest temperatures reached are shown by two small indicators, which are moved by a thread of mercury, and stay in position so that a reading can be taken. They are then reset with a magnet.

Temperature at higher levels is measured by thermometers attached to balloons, which rise to ten thousand feet or more. A continuous record of the temperature can be kept with a *thermograph* (2). This is a special type of thermometer which operates a pen moving over paper fixed to a slowly revolving drum which turns completely in seven days. These thermometers, and the other instruments like the Barograph, which is a recording barometer (1), and another type of hygrometer (3), are housed in a special slatted box called a *Stevenson Screen*.

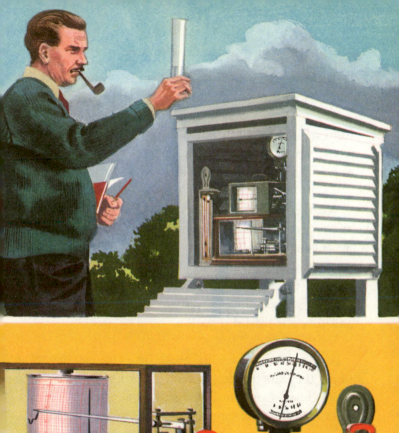

Building the Weather Picture

Before a meteorologist can forecast the weather he must know the conditions over a very wide area. He makes his 'big picture' from information sent to him from weather stations scattered far and wide, from the Arctic wastes to the distant parts of the ocean, as well as from towns and villages inland.

Weather information is collected in weather stations on desolate islands, on headlands and mountains, from weather ships far out on the ocean and from aircraft on set meteorological flights. The observations are made both by professional and amateur meteorologists, and often by school-children who have learned how to collect and forward the information.

All these observations must be made at the same time; they are made, in fact, at 9.0 a.m. Greenwich mean time. They must also be sent at once to a central point where the information can be plotted on a map, to make the 'big picture'. This was not possible, of course, until the telegraph, telephone, and, best of all, radio were available.

The information is studied and compared with the conditions twenty-four hours previously, and from this the skilled meteorologist can, by his knowledge and experience, forecast the probable trend of the weather in the next twenty-four hours.

The Weather Map

The first thing you notice on this typical weather map is the "LOW" over Wales. This is the centre of a region of low pressure, or a depression. The three rings round the "LOW", and the thin lines in the bottom corners, are *isobars*, which are lines drawn on the map joining places having the same atmospheric pressure at the same time. They are like contour lines on a map which join places of the same height.

Each isobar is marked with the height of the barometer in inches, and another figure, for example on the third ring 1004 mb. The letters "mb" stand for millibars which are the units the meteorologist uses to measure atmospheric pressure. Following round the third ring you will see that 1004 mb. equals 29.65 inches.

As we saw on page 20 winds blow anti-clockwise round and into low pressure areas. On the map these winds, with their speeds in miles per hour, and their directions, are shown thus ㉒:

You can also see two heavy lines, one with spikes and the other with half-circles. These are *fronts;* the spikes indicating a *cold front* and the half-circles a *warm front*. Very simply a cold front means colder air moving in the direction of the spikes, and a warm front warmer air moving in the direction of the half-circles. The figures not in rings show air temperatures and you can see how these differ on either side of the fronts.

The study of this map, which gives the weather conditions on one particular day in July only, will help you to understand other weather maps which are published every day.

GENERAL FORECAST

A vigorous depression is expected to move from e Atlantic towards the Bristol Channel. England d Wales will have mostly cloudy weather, with ain in many areas, but especially in the W. and N., where it will be heavy at times. Later in day winds may reach gale force in W. districts. S. Scotland and Northern Ireland are expected to be mostly cloudy, with rain at times and E. winds which will become strong in places. Central and N. districts of Scotland seem likely to have bright intervals and only scattered showers.

Weather Sayings

Weather sayings have been used from ancient times, and handed down through the generations. How do their predictions compare with the scientific forecasting of to-day? The great drawback of this traditional forecasting is that the observer can only judge from what he sees about him, whereas the meteorologist can see the 'big picture'. So most of these sayings are very local.

Perhaps the best known of the general sayings is— "A red sky at night is the shepherd's delight. A red sky in the morning is the shepherd's warning." The trouble with this is that it all depends on what kind of a red sky there is at sunset: some do, indeed, imply a fine day to follow, but some do not. If it rains on July 15th, St. Swithin's Day, it is supposed to rain for the next forty days. Rainfall records over sixty years have proved that there is no truth in this legend.

Animals, birds and some flowers, certainly react to change in the weather and many old sayings are based on their behaviour. The Scarlet Pimpernel, for example, is called 'the poor man's weather glass' because its petals stay closed in cool weather.

The rainbow has given rise to many weather sayings, in which there is often some truth. It is also the subject of the oldest weather saying of all. In Genesis we read that God set the rainbow in the sky as a promise to Noah that there would never be another great flood.